MORE THAN JUST FOOTBALL

TEAMWORK, CHARACTER AND RESPECT ON THE PITCH

Matt Scheff

raintree

a Capstone company — publishers for children

Raintree is an imprint of Capstone Global Library Limited, a company incorporated in England and Wales having its registered office at 264 Banbury Road, Oxford, OX2 7DY – Registered company number: 6695582

www.raintree.co.uk
myorders@raintree.co.uk

Edited by Alison Deering
Designed by Heidi Thompson

Media research by Morgan Walters
Original illustrations © Capstone Global Library Limited
Originated by Capstone Global Library Ltd
Production by Tori Abraham

978 1 3982 3380 5 (hardback)
978 1 3982 3381 2 (paperback)

British Library Cataloguing in Publication Data
A full catalogue record for this book is available from the

Acknowledgements
We would like to thank the following for permission to reproduce photographs: Alamy: PA Images, 11; Associated Press: Dean Mouhtaropoulos, 24; Getty Images: Gareth Copley/Staff, 29, Gary M. Prior/Staff, 13, Mike Hewitt/Staff, 7, MOHAMMED MAHJOUB/Stringer, 14, 15, sampics/Contributor, 21; iStockphoto: PeopleImages, Cover, (right top), skynesher, Cover, (right bottom); Newscom: AFLO/Maurizio Borsari, 28, Bennett Cohen/ZUMA Press, Cover, 4, EFE/Javiar Lizon, 22, Icon SportswireDHZ/Brian Rotmuller, 9, picture-alliance/dpa/Marius Becker, 17, Reuters/MUHAMMAD HAMED, 19, ZUMA Press/Jed Leicester, 23, ZUMA Press/Matthew impey, 10; Shutterstock: Avector, (dots) design element, Hafiz Johari, 6, irin-k (soccer ball) design element, Jacob Lund, Cover, (right middle), Jose Breton- Pics Action, 8, S_Photo (pitch) design element; Sports Illustrated: Al Tielemans, 27, Simon Bruty, 26

Printed and bound in India.

Richmond upon Thames Libraries

Renew online at www.richmond.gov.uk/libraries

LONDON BOROUGH OF
RICHMOND UPON THAMES

CONTENTS

Glossary terms are **BOLD** on first use.

TEAMWORK, CHARACTER AND RESPECT

Football is the world's most popular sport. Fans love watching their favourite players thread passes and blast shots at goal. But sometimes, football is about more than scoring goals. It's about fair play, compassion and setting a good example.

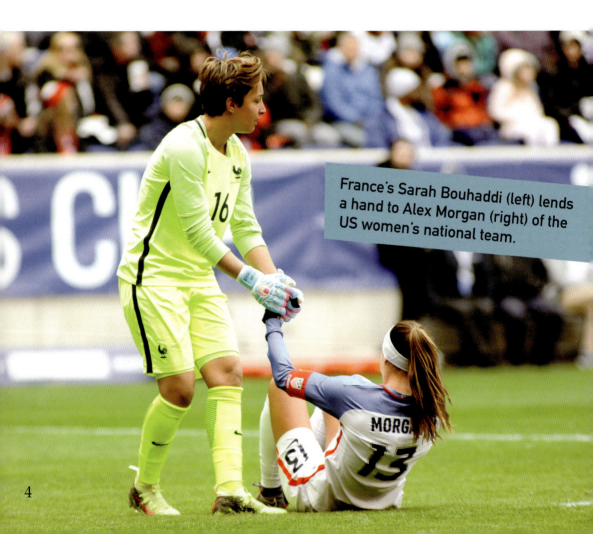

France's Sarah Bouhaddi (left) lends a hand to Alex Morgan (right) of the US women's national team.

Players come together during a match.

Sportsmanship, character and respect on the pitch tell a lot about a player or a team. Players help each other up after a fall. They congratulate each other after a great performance. They exchange shirts after matches. And they offer support to both teammates and opponents.

How players behave on and off the pitch is just as important as results and statistics. It's all about doing the right thing and setting an example for all to follow.

SETTING AN EXAMPLE

In Premier League football, winning is a big deal. But for many teams and players, it's about more than that. It's also about fair play.

Looking out for an opponent

In December 2000, Everton and West Ham United were locked in a 1–1 draw. Late in the match, Everton's goalkeeper, Paul Gerrard, hurt his knee as he went to defend a West Ham attack. Play continued as Gerrard lay on the ground. He was in pain.

West Ham forward Paolo Di Canio received a pass near the goal. It was a chance to score an easy goal to end the deadlock. It could have been West Ham's chance to win the game.

But Di Canio didn't take the shot. Instead, he caught the ball. That caused play to stop so that Gerrard could get medical help. It was a show of **empathy** and compassion for a fellow player and a true display of sportsmanship.

West Ham's Paolo Di Canio (right) receives a special award for sportsmanship from Paul Gerrard (left) of Everton.

Showing the way

When it comes to teamwork, it's hard to top the 2019 United States women's national team. The United States dominated the Women's World Cup. They used **precision** passing, electric goal-scoring and firm defending to win all of their matches on the way to the title.

The popularity of women's football in the United States had been on the rise for decades. But the amazing teamwork of the 2019 team took it to a new level. They set an example for young athletes everywhere. They showed that with teamwork, anything is possible.

The United States celebrated after winning the final match of the FIFA Women's World Cup in 2019.

Fans supported the ongoing fight for equal pay during the USA Victory Tour match between the United States and the Republic of Ireland in 2019.

The American women's team players also fought for equal pay with men, who earned far more money for playing for the national team. It was a demand for respect that was hard to ignore.

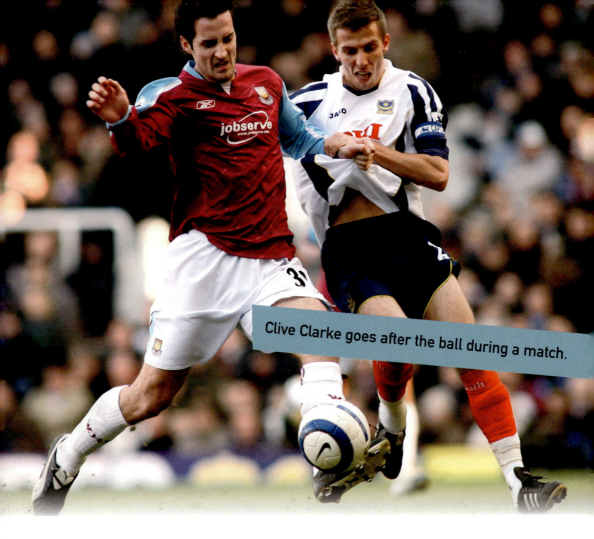

Clive Clarke goes after the ball during a match.

Fair play

In 2007, Leicester and Nottingham Forest faced off in a match. Nottingham Forest took control in the first half. They led 1–0 at half time. But during the break, Leicester's Clive Clarke collapsed in the locker room. It was a heart attack – a serious medical problem. The match was called off.

Thankfully, Clarke survived. The match was replayed a few weeks later. It started again at 0–0. But Leicester knew that Forest had earned a lead. They made the surprising decision to let Forest score a goal to start the match. That reset the score at 1–0.

In a sport where teams go all out to win, Leicester showed that sometimes fairness was more important.

Nottingham Forest's manager, Colin Calderwood, speaks to the crowd.

Getting it right

The stakes were high when Liverpool and Arsenal played each other in 1997. Winning was important to Liverpool's Robbie Fowler. But he wanted to do it in the right way. When Fowler fell near the Arsenal goal, an official signalled that Fowler had been fouled by the goalkeeper.

Fowler knew that he hadn't been tripped. He'd just fallen. He told the official, but the foul stood. Fowler was awarded a penalty kick, but his kick was weak. It looked like Fowler hadn't even tried to score.

Fowler denied that he'd missed on purpose, but the truth was clear to anyone watching. Fowler hadn't wanted to score a penalty he didn't deserve. His act of sportsmanship didn't cost his team. Liverpool won the match 2–1. And they did it without the benefit of a bad decision.

The shirt exchange

Exchanging football shirts after a match is a football tradition. In a show of sportsmanship and respect, players often meet at the end of the match to talk and swap shirts. It's a way to connect with opponents in a warm and friendly way. Many football stars treasure their collection of opponent's shirts.

Tony Adams (left) of Arsenal grabs the shirt of Liverpool's Robbie Fowler (right).

Tied up

In November 2013, Al-Nahda and Al-Ittihad were locked in a tight 2–2 Saudi Premier League match. After taking a pass, Al-Nahda's goalkeeper Taisir Al Antaif realized that his boot was untied. Goalkeepers wear large gloves, meaning Al Antaif would be unable to tie his own boot.

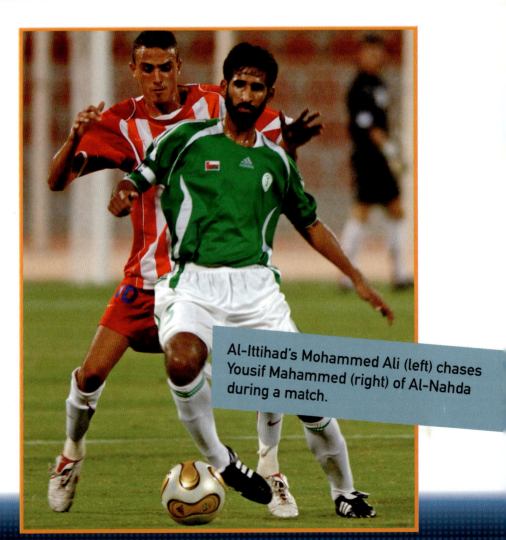

Al-Ittihad's Mohammed Ali (left) chases Yousif Mahammed (right) of Al-Nahda during a match.

Majid Salim (left) of Al-Nahda and Akram Abbad (right) of Al-Ittihad fight for control of the ball.

Al-Ittihad striker Jobson noticed the problem. He ran over and tied Al Antaif's laces for him. An official thought the goalkeeper was wasting time, however, and blew for a foul.

Al-Ittihad had no interest in taking advantage of this mistake. They booted the ball out of play from the free kick. The match was restarted, and play continued, eventually ending in a 4–4 draw. It was a show of empathy and sportsmanship that gained worldwide attention.

SHOWING SUPPORT

Football can be a hard sport. Sometimes it takes the support of teammates – or opponents – to get through a tough time. Whether it's personal tragedy or just a bad day, a show of support can make all the difference.

Paying tribute

Winger James Rodríguez was a superstar for Colombia's national team in the 2014 World Cup. He scored six goals in the tournament and carried his team. Still, Colombia were no match for Brazil in the quarter-finals. They were defeated 2–1.

Rodríguez was emotional as the final minutes ticked away. All his hard work hadn't been enough. Brazil's David Luiz saw his opponent's pain. He approached Rodríguez and waved towards the crowd asking them to cheer.

The crowd did just that. They rose to their feet and gave Rodríguez a huge **ovation**. Luiz's show of empathy didn't take away the sting of losing. But it helped Rodríguez walk off the field a winner in his own way.

Brazil's David Luiz (left) comforted opponent James Rodríguez (right) of Colombia following a 2014 FIFA World Cup match.

Building a wall

The game isn't always the biggest thing on the line in football. That was true when Shabab al Ordon Club faced Arab Orthodox Club (AOC) in the 2017 West Asian Football Federation Women's Championship.

During the match, an AOC player realized that her **hijab** was slipping off her head. In the Islamic faith, a hijab is an important head covering for a woman. It's part of the culture for a woman to cover her head and hair. Having it fall off would have been embarrassing or even shameful.

The AOC player slowed as she tried to fix the hijab. Shabab's players saw what was happening and understood. Instead of continuing play, they formed a human wall, providing their opponent privacy as she fixed the hijab. Their show of empathy and compassion became a **social media** sensation.

Shabab al Ordon players warm up before a match in Amman, Jordan.

Reaching out

Bayern Munich and Valencia were locked in a tight battle in the UEFA Champions League 2000–2001. It was a contest between great goalkeepers. Santiago Canizares was a star for Valencia. Bayern Munich's Oliver Kahn was famous for his great skill – and his big heart. Both were on display in the final moments of the big match.

The match was tied 1–1 after extra time. That meant penalty kicks would decide the winner. Kahn made a huge save and clinched the match for Bayern. Canizares dropped to the ground in disappointment as the Bayern players celebrated.

The Fair Play Code

FIFA, the organizing body for international football, has a Fair Play Code that it expects players to honour. The code includes ten rules of fair play.

1. Play to win.
2. Accept defeat with dignity.
3. Observe the laws of the game.
4. Respect opponents, teammates, referees, officials and spectators.
5. Promote the interests of football.
6. Honour those who defend football's good reputation.
7. Reject corruption, drugs, racism, violence, gambling and dangers to the sport.
8. Help others reject corruption.
9. Speak out against those who cheat.
10. Use football to make a better world.

But Kahn didn't join in. Instead, he rushed over to Canizares. It was an inspiring act of compassion and sportsmanship. It was more important to Kahn to show concern for a friend and competitor than it was to celebrate.

Oliver Kahn (left) comforts Santiago Canizares (right).

A show of support

Real Madrid are Barcelona's biggest **rivals**. But that didn't stop the team from showing their support for their rivals during a difficult time. In 2012, Barcelona's Eric Abidal was going through a health crisis. He needed an emergency liver **transplant**. It was a big deal, and no one knew how it would turn out.

Real Madrid players wear T-shirts in support of Barcelona's defender Eric Abidal.

In a show of support, Real Madrid players wore T-shirts that read *Animo Abidal* or *Soul Abidal* before a March 2012 match. Other T-shirts said *Get well soon Muamba*. That was for Fabrice Muamba, a player from Bolton Wanderers. Muamba had collapsed on the field the day before due to a heart attack.

The Real Madrid players were showing empathy for two fellow players going through tough times. They proved that compassion can come before competition.

West Ham United's Kevin Nolan (left) and Carlton Cole (right) wear T-shirts for Barcelona's Eric Abidal and Bolton's Fabrice Muamba.

MORE THAN A GAME

Sometimes football is bigger than just the match. It's about social and global issues. It's a chance for teams and players to lead and set an example.

Players from the US women's team wore *Black Lives Matter* shirts ahead of a match against the Netherlands in November 2020.

Standing up

In 2020, **social justice** was on the minds of many players. Following the deaths of George Floyd, Breonna Taylor and other Black men and women in the United States, members of the National Women's Soccer League wanted to speak out. They wanted to lead.

The US women's national team wore T-shirts with the words *Black Lives Matter* on them before their first match of the Challenge Cup in June 2020. It was a slogan representing the fight for social justice. In November 2020, they wore *Black Lives Matter* warm-up tops ahead of their match against the Netherlands.

Many players also posted a joint statement on their social media accounts. "We love our country, and it is a true honour to represent America. It is also our duty to demand that the liberties and freedoms that our country was founded on extend to everyone."

Peace over politics

Tensions between the United States and Iran were high when the two teams met at the 1998 World Cup. Violence had broken out between the two nations. No one was sure what to expect at the match. The host country, France, feared that the tension could boil over. French officials had extra security at the match.

But there was no reason to worry. The US and Iranian players showed that peace was the better way. The players from Iran gifted their American opponents with white roses before the match. White roses are a symbol of peace. Then the players all gathered to pose for photographs.

Iran ultimately came out on top, 2–1. But in this match, everyone left feeling good about themselves.

Players from the United States and Iran posed together at the 1998 World Cup.

Frankie Hejduk (left) of the United States and Iran's Mehrdad Minavand (right) in action during the 1998 World Cup.

Acting fast

Footballers have to think and act quickly. But that took on new meaning in a March 2014 match between Dynamo Kiev and Dnipro. Dynamo Kiev's captain, Oleg Gusev, collapsed on the field after a collision with another player. Gusev had swallowed his own tongue. He was choking.

Dnipro midfielder Jaba Kankava rushed to Gusev's side. He stuck his hand down Gusev's throat to clear his airway. Sports aren't usually life-or-death situations. But this time it was Kankava's quick action that probably saved his opponent's life.

Dnipro midfielder Jaba Kankava

Dynamo Kiev's captain, Oleg Gusev, in action in 2015.

Kankava was a hero. He showed that teamwork didn't just extend to players wearing the same shirts. It's about looking out for everyone – teammates and opponents alike – and using football as a way to lead and set an example that anyone can follow.

GLOSSARY

empathy imagining or feeling how others feel

hijab traditional covering for the hair and neck that is worn by Muslim women

ovation expression of approval or enthusiasm made by clapping or cheering

precision with exact accuracy

rival person or team with whom one has an especially intense competition

social justice equality and fairness for all people in a society

social media forms of electronic communication, such as websites, through which people create online communities to share information, ideas and personal messages

transplant operation in which a diseased organ is replaced with a healthy one

FIND OUT MORE

BOOKS

Football School Terrific Teams: 50 True Stories of Football's Greatest Sides, Alex Bellos and Ben Lyttleton (Walker Books, 2021)

Play Like Your Football Heroes: Pro Tips for Becoming a Top Player, Seth Burkett and Matt Oldfield (Walker Books, 2021)

Unbelievable Football 2: How Football Can Change the World, Matt Oldfield (Wren & Rook, 2021)

WEBSITES

www.bbc.co.uk/sport/37405389
Read this BBC article about the best examples of sportsmanship shown between athletes.

www.dkfindout.com/uk/sports/football/
Find out more about football with DKfindout!

INDEX